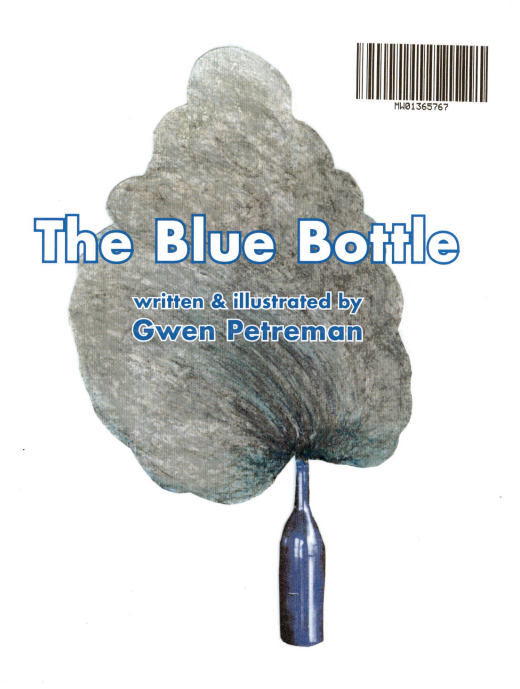

# The Blue Bottle

### written & illustrated by
### Gwen Petreman

This book is dedicated to Dan, Jeff and Michelle.

Thanks to Miles Sullivan for contributing helpful ideas when illustrating the monster.

A special thank you is extended to Sarah Hamilton-Wright for her contributions.

**Visit Gwen Petreman at: apluslearningmaterials.com**

Order this book online at www.trafford.com, or email orders@trafford.com

Most Trafford titles are also available at major online book retailers.

© Copyright 2010 A+ Learning Materials.

All rights reserved. No part of this publication may be reproduced, stored in a retrieval system, or transmitted, in any form or by any means, electronic, mechanical, photocopying, recording, or otherwise, without the written prior permission of the author.

Teachers have permission to copy response pages at the back.

Printed in Victoria, BC, Canada. ISBN: 978-1-4269-0298-7

*We at Trafford believe that it is the responsibility of us all, as both individuals and corporations, to make choices that are environmentally and socially sound. You, in turn, are supporting this responsible conduct each time you purchase a Trafford book, or make use of our publishing services. To find out how you are helping, please visit www.trafford.com/responsiblepublishing.html*

*Our mission is to efficiently provide the world's finest, most comprehensive book publishing service, enabling every author to experience success. To find out how to publish your book, your way, and have it available worldwide, visit us online at www.trafford.com*

*Trafford rev: 12/21/2009*

www.trafford.com

**North America & international**
toll-free: 1 888 232 4444 (USA & Canada)
phone: 250 383 6864 ♦ fax: 812 355 4082
email: info@trafford.com

Rose Larsen lived all by herself in a colorful house at the edge of a woodland. She loved her gardens and she especially loved the woods behind her house. Rose hated to waste anything. One of her favorite days was curb rescue. On that day everyone in the little town close to her house would put items out on the curb that they no longer wanted.

On Monday morning Rose woke up earlier than usual. Today was curb rescue. She hoped she would find some vases for the oxeye daisies growing in her garden.

At one of the houses Rose found a lovely box, just the right size for her vegetable seeds. A few minutes later Rose beamed when she spied a blue bottle. It was rather grimy looking, but after a good cleaning, she could just imagine how lovely it would look with a bouquet of daisies.

She hurried home with her treasures. After lunch, Rose went out on her deck to clean out the bottle. Just as she pulled her brush out of the bottle, big billows of black smoke poured out. Rose stared in disbelief at the sight that appeared before her. There in front of her, staring wildly from his blood-filled eyes towered a massive monster!

His whole body was covered with layers and layers of prickly, black scales. At the end of his huge and scaly arms hung hands as big as shovels. Dirty steel-like nails protruded from his grimy fingers.

"Free! Free! I'm finally free! Now I can begin my work!" roared the monster.

"What-what do you mean your work? What do you do?" asked Rose in a trembling voice.

"I go around the world and rip trees right out of the ground! Do you know what my first job will be?" roared the monster.

"N-N-No I don't," stammered Rose.

"My first job, little lady, will be to destroy all the trees in the woods behind your house!" laughed the monster.

"Why would you want to do such a terrible thing? If you destroy all the trees in the world the forests will turn into deserts!" cried Rose.

"PERFECT! JUST PERFECT! That's exactly what I want. I love hot and dry deserts. I love prickly cactus plants. My favorite snacks are scorpions and tarantulas. After I've ripped out all your trees, I am heading south to the Amazon rain forest! The sooner I destroy the Amazon rain forest, the happier I'll be. I hate rain forests!" sneered the monster.

"But—but if you destroy the rain forests all the animals that live in them will die! They can't suddenly survive in a desert, no matter how hard they try," protested Rose.

"I don't care about those animals. I only care about me. I do what I want," thundered the monster.

"But-but we need trees! They give us oxygen. They give us fruits and nuts and lumber for our houses and-and all kinds of paper. And many animals need trees to live in. And we need trees to suck up pollution like-like green house gases!" cried Rose in an exasperated voice.

"Lady, weren't you listening? I already told you, I DON'T CARE! Now make your three wishes so I can get out of here!" bellowed the monster.

"What are you talking about?" asked Rose.

"Well, there is this rule that says I can't leave until I have granted three wishes to the person who frees me from the bottle. Since you let me out of the bottle you have to make three wishes. And by the way, your wishes must involve fame and fortune," explained the monster.

"I don't want any of your wishes," cried Rose. "I don't want to be famous! I don't want to be rich!"

"You must be kidding! What's the matter with you lady? Everybody wants to be rich! Everybody wants to be famous! You have to make three wishes. If you do not make three wishes I cannot leave! I will destroy all the trees behind your house and you will have to spend the rest of your life in a desert- with ME!" roared the monster.

Rose was horrified. She didn't know what to do. She thought and thought and thought and finally she cried, "Okay, I have my three wishes!"

"It's about time! I want to get out of here! RIGHT NOW!" roared the monster.

"Well, for my first wish, I want YOU-to become rich. For my second wish, I want YOU-to become famous," replied Rose.

"What kind of crazy fool are you? You want ME to become rich and famous? Ha! Ha! Ha! You really are weird!" laughed the monster in disbelief.

Rose continued...

"And for my third wish, I want YOU-to become-my-son."

Immediately, the monster disappeared behind a huge plume of black

smoke. Rose could hear the monster howling, "No! No! No! What-have-you-done? What is happening to-me?"

Then suddenly the smoke began to change colors. It went from flaming red, to vibrant yellow and finally, a brilliant blue. Suddenly, the colors started to swirl around and around. Through the swirling colors of smoke Rose could see the monster's black, scaly legs.

"Oh no!" she murmured to herself. "Don't tell me that terrifying creature is back!"

She thought she heard someone calling. Rose stared in disbelief! Appearing out of the billows of smoke and walking towards her was a serious looking young man with metal-framed glasses. The next thing she knew the young man ran right up to her and gave her a big hug.

"Hey Mom! I have the best news ever! I am getting 1.3 million dollars!" cried the young man.

"I don't understand. Who in the world would give you that kind of money?" asked Rose.

"I won the Nobel Prize for all the research I did on climate change and the Amazon rain forest! I was so excited I couldn't sleep a wink last night. And you will never guess who called me early this morning. The President of Brazil called ME-David Larsen. And do you know why he called me? He wants me to come up with a plan to help save the Amazon rain forest. I need all kinds of volunteers to help me! How about it Mom, would you like to come with me to work in the Amazon rain forest?" asked David.

"I have always wanted to go to the Amazon rain forest!" beamed Rose.

In her mind's eye Rose imagined what she might see in the rain forest.

"I hope I get to see an adorable, little brocket deer and a sloth," declared Rose.

"I'm sure you will! And I hope I get to see an anaconda and a jaguar. Oh, I almost forgot! I brought you a bouquet of daisies," cried David.

"Let me put the daisies in water before they wilt," replied Rose. She took the bouquet and tucked it into the blue bottle.

With a very puzzled look, David stared at the bottle. "I really like your blue bottle Mom. I haven't seen it before. Did you just get it?" asked David.

"Yes, I did. And it was a very, very lucky find," smiled Rose.

### THE END

# Choose five animals and find five facts about each one.

# How Can I Help Preserve Trees?

1. Plant as many trees as possible on your property.
2. Get involved in community tree planting projects.
3. Never pull the bark off trees as that will kill them.
4. Help your mom and dad water trees on your property and on the boulevard.
5. Use recycled toilet paper, napkins, and paper towels.
6. Whenever possible, use a rag instead of paper towels.
7. When printing, use both sides of the paper.
8. Use every part of all white paper, before recycling, such as practicing spelling words on the blank spaces of the paper.
9. Instead of sending Christmas cards, send an email greeting with free clip art from the internet.
10. Use reusable gift bags for presents.

# How Can I Help Protect Animals in the Amazon Rain Forest?

The World Wildlife Federation has all kinds of programs to help protect animal species around the world. They have a variety of on-going projects including an Animal Adoption Program whereby you donate a specific amount of money to WWF. The money is used to save some of the most endangered species from extinction and helps to support WWF's conservation efforts. When you make a donation, check the website to see what you might receive. Usually, you get a plush toy of your adopted animal, a photo and an adoption certificate. Check www.worldwildlife.org to learn more about how you can help protect the Amazon rain forest.

# Trees —Did You Know?

1. Since the beginning of time trees have provided humans with fiber-rich fruits, protein-laden nuts, shelter, timber, firewood, medicines, and protection from predators and the weather.
2. Of all the plants on Earth, trees live the longest and serve more uses than any other plant.
3. Trees provide habitats for all kinds of animals.
4. All aquatic life in our lakes begin their life cycles along the lake shore. Trees and shrubs planted along the lake shore provide shade for the fragile beginnings of eggs from fish and other aquatic creatures which would otherwise perish from the intense rays of the sun.
5. During photosynthesis, trees absorb carbon dioxide, a major greenhouse gas, while providing us with oxygen.
6. Trees store millions of tons of carbon and other pollutants such as nitrogen oxides, sulphur dioxides, and particulates associated with breathing problems.

7. The roots of trees help clean the water by absorbing chemicals and heavy metals.
8. The roots of trees will not grow into drain pipes, unless the pipes are cracked.
9. Planting trees in parking lots can prevent cars left in the sun from emitting their own blend of pollutants into the air.
10. The roots of trees help to stabilize the soil, preventing fertile soil from blowing away.
11. The roots of one mature tree can hold staggering amounts of water. Planting trees on hillsides will help reduce or even prevent mudslides during flash floods.
12. Streets that are lined with mature trees are cooler in summer than streets with no trees.
13. In summer, mature trees growing in the front and back yard can reduce the use of an air conditioner and help save money.
14. In winter, evergreen trees can act as windbreaks; consequently, lowering heating bills.

# Tremendous Trees

## Maple Trees

When it comes to beauty and a show of color *maple trees* are probably the most admired in North America. At least one species of maple trees grows naturally in every province of Canada and in every state of United States. Although maple trees grow all over the world, maple syrup is made only in Canada and United States. The sap from sugar maples is boiled to produce maple syrup. If the sap is boiled long enough it will become maple sugar. Native people were producing maple syrup long before the Pilgrims arrived in America in 1620. Not only do sugar maples produce sap, but they support hundreds of different animals. Birds, insects, and mammals such as squirrels, deer, raccoons, and porcupines rely on maples for food and shelter. Voles and mice store maple seeds for winter food. Sugar maples are fast growing and the timber can be used for pulp, board, and firewood. Due to the hardness of the wood it is used for making ten-pin-bowling pins.

## Oak Trees

Many people consider the *oak tree* to be one of the most magnificent trees to behold. There are more than 300 species of oak trees. It is able to grow on the thinnest soil and on top of mountains. It can tolerate salt and will thrive in the sun or full shade. Since oak is a beautiful and very durable hardwood it has been used to build navies, cathedrals and cities. The great Gothic cathedrals in Europe used oak to hold up the roofs and create the immense doors. Oak was also used for the vaulted roofs since it is fire-resistant. The Mayflower ship which brought the Pilgrims to America was built from oak.

A single oak tree can provide food and shelter for over 300 species of animals including insects. The jays depend on the oak tree for their winter food. As jays forget where they have stored their larder of acorns for the winter, new oak trees grow from the forgotten acorns in the spring. Today, we think of the acorn as food for animals; however, in the past, before crops were planted, the acorn was ground down and added to cereals. It was also made into dough and used to make bread.

## Pine Trees

There are about 115 species of *pine trees* and there are about 35 species found in North America. Pines are evergreen trees that can grow to be between 15-45 meters (50-145 feet) tall. The seeds of pines are commonly eaten by birds and squirrels. Some birds distribute the seeds to new areas. The pine needles are eaten by the caterpillars of some butterflies and moths. Throughout the world pine trees are valued for their timber and wood pulp. Pine wood is used in carpentry items such as floors, window frames, and furniture. The resin of some pine trees is used to make turpentine. Pine trees are very popular as ornamental trees in public parks, gardens and residential properties. Pine trees are also commercially grown and harvested for Christmas trees. Some pine trees have large seeds called pine nuts which are used for cooking and baking. You can soak young green pine needles in boiling water and make a tea that is high in Vitamins A and C.

The tallest pines are the *sugar pines* that often reach heights of 61 meters (200 feet). Sugar pines are also one of the longest living pines. Sugar pines can live up to 500 years. The cones of the sugar pines are the largest in the world and may exceed 60 cm (2 feet) in length. In the past, the sugar pine was important to indigenous people. They used the seeds and bark for food, the rootlets for baskets, the pitch for glue to repair canoes and fasten arrowheads and feathers to shafts, and the needles and bark for medicinal teas. They drank the sugar pine sap, harvested and ate the seeds from the cones.

The oldest pines are *bristlecone pines*. One of the bristlecone pines located in the Ancient Bristlecone Pine Forest in California is believed to be the oldest living organism in the world. In 2008 it was 4,840 years old!

## Spruce Trees

In Scandinavia and Eastern Russia, the *Norway spruce* is the main tree grown for timber. In Canada and United States it is the *white spruce* and in parts of central Europe it is the *Sitka spruce*. The spruce's timber is converted into many products such as chipboard, hardboard, cardboard, and packaging materials. Spruce wood also called whitewood, is used to make many musical instruments. Along with other trees, spruce is used to make writing paper, printer paper and food cartons. The spruce's resin is used to make turpentine.

Native people in North America used white spruce for snowshoe frames, bows, pots, and trays. They used the decayed wood for tanning animal hides. The sap was heated to make glue to fasten arrowheads onto shafts. The spruce needles which are high in Vitamin C can be boiled into a tea and are useful in survival situations. Early explorers in North America used the needles to prevent scurvy.

## Redwood Trees

The tallest trees in the world are the *redwood trees*. They can grow to be about 105 meters (345 feet) tall. They grow in California and Oregon in the United States. Some redwood trees are over 2,000 years old! One mature redwood tree is so big that it can provide enough timber to make 35 houses, each one big enough for a family of four.

# Banyan Trees

The *banyan tree* is a very unusual fig tree that sends shoots from its branches which take root and grow new trunks. They can be found in almost every village in India. The largest known banyan tree can be found on the island of Sri Lanka. It has 350 large trunks and over 3,000 smaller ones.

# Mangrove Swamps

The coastlines of more than 80 countries around the world contain vast stretches of tropical forests known as *mangrove swamps.* The mangrove swamps offer excellent defense against hurricanes and cyclones. Unfortunately, countless mangrove swamps have been destroyed to create huge shrimp farms. In 1999, when a super cyclone hit the coast below West Bengal, where the mangrove swamps had been destroyed, more than ten thousand people were killed and 7 million were left homeless. However, the villages located near the country's second largest mangrove swamp reported no deaths. The mangrove swamps had protected them from the deathly cyclone.

# Coconut Palm Trees

The *coconut palm tree* has long had the reputation of being able to serve all the necessities of life. It can withstand powerful storms and grow in salty sand. Coconuts can float for up to a year on the salty ocean and then can sprout beautifully when planted in pure sand. The 30 meter (98 foot) trunk of the coconut palm tree is used for furniture, drums, containers, small bridges, and small canoes. The leaves are used for baskets and roofing thatch. The stiff leaflet midribs are bound into bundles to make brooms and brushes. The coconut shells can be used to make cups, bowls and jewelry. Dried half coconut shells with husks are used to buff floors. The husks and shells are a good source of charcoal. In the Philippines dried half shells are used as musical instruments and they are also used for sound effects in movies. Shirt buttons can be carved out of dried coconut shells. The coir fibers are used to make ropes, mats, brushes, caulking boats and making potting compost. The fleshy part of the coconut is used in cooking. Coconut milk is made by processing grated coconut with hot water or milk. The leftover fiber from coconut milk production is used for livestock feed. Coconut water found in the cavity is highly nutritious and is used as a refreshing drink. Coconut oil is used in medicines and cosmetics. The roots are used as a dye, a mouthwash and a medicine for dysentery.

# Olive Trees

The *olive tree* has more than 500 species and has been cultivated for more than ten thousand years! Olive trees can grow olives for more than a thousand years! Olive trees are native to the Mediterranean, Asia and parts of Africa. They can grow in hot, harsh conditions where the soil is dry and dusty. Olive trees have been cultivated since ancient times as a source of olive oil, fine wood, olives for eating, and leaves for making medicinal tea.

## Fruit Trees

Fruits are a vital source of food for people and animals. In order to maintain optimum health, nutritionists recommend that we eat fruit every day. Most fruits grow on trees. The most popular fruits grown in the world are citrus fruits, bananas, cherries, pears, plums, and apples. Apples have nourished people and animals for over ten thousand years. It is believed that they originated in Kazakhstan and are now grown around the world. Apple trees have thrived because they can tolerate many different temperatures and can grow well in many soil types. Apples are great at staying fresh and holding their nutritional value for long periods of storage. Some varieties of apples can last right through winter. Apples can be eaten raw or cooked to make sauces, jams and jellies and they can be made into a number of drinks such as apples juice and apple cider.

## Rubber Trees

*Rubber trees* grow in the rain forests of South America. The sap inside the rubber tree is called latex. The latex is used to make rubber products such as tires, rubber balls, rubber hoses, rubber boots, and running shoes.

## Cacao Trees

The *cacao tree* grows in the rain forests of South America. Cacao flowers grow right out of the tree trunks. The flowers turn into cacao pods. The seeds or beans inside are used to make chocolate.

## Nut Trees

Nuts from nut trees provide us with a good source of protein. The Brazil nut is one kind of nut harvested from trees that grow wild in the rain forest. These trees can grow to be more than 50 meters (164 feet) tall and may live to be 500 years or more. If people try to remove Brazil nut trees from the rain forest they will not be found by a small bee. If the flowers are not pollinated by these tiny bees, the tree will not bear any Brazil nuts. Between 12-25 Brazil nuts grow inside a large pod which may weigh up to 2 kilograms (4 pounds). A rain forest animal called an agouti uses its razor sharp teeth to open the pod. The agouti will then bury the nuts throughout the rain forest and in 12 to 18 months they will begin to germinate. In order for people to open a Brazil nut, they need a nutcracker. The people who live in the rain forest eat the nuts raw and mix them with manioc flour.